Edgar Allan Poe's Christmas by Mark Ncube age 11

Once upon a midnight cheery, while I waited tired and weary
By the fireplace as I'd done on Christmases before
While I nodded, nearly napping, suddenly there came a tapping
As of reindeer gently rapping,
Rapping atop the highest floor.
As I whispered quietly "IT'S HIM!!!"
Or perhaps I screamed it like a boar.
Time to get my gifts galore.

Yes, distinctly I remember,
'Twas the 24th of December
And I had just sent several letters saying
I had been good the year before.
Eagerly I wished the morrow;
No more would I have to sorrow,
For I had wished the perfect gift
That no one else had wished before.
Most toy retailers have many choices
I could surely not ignore
So, I requested every store.

Filled with wonderful elation
Patiently waiting with anticipation
By the fireplace, until I heard a knock upon the door
"That was odd?" I thought confused,
Why would Santa use the door?
Right! I recalled

This chimney is fake and
Simply set up for décor
In fact, it plugs into the floor.

If I had been a slightly stronger,
I'd have waited a slightly longer
But I wanted my gifts, right there, right now so I ran to reach the door!
Once he had stepped foot inside,
I'd offer him a cookie bribe
And stand and watch as he supplied
The many gifts I'd humbly asked before.

Here I opened wide the door…
Darkness there, and nothing more.
Back into the chamber turning,
All my Christmas spirit burning.
"Holy snickerdoodle!" I did implore
As I lay prostrate on the floor.
Saint Nicholas was behind my door.
"Surely couldn't you have waited
Outside the chamber door?"

"No matter," I said
"I won't keep you long,
Just leave the gifts and hum a song,
For I know you have
A long and busy night in store."
With one single gift he replied:
"Less is more."

“Um?” I said, “I disagree.”
Trying not to let him see
That what I wanted most for me
Wasn’t toys from the First World War.
I didn’t want one lousy gift,
I wanted the ENTIRE STORE
So, I contended back: “more is more!”
Then Father Christmas, condescending,
His lame and pithy gift, rescinding
Took that stupid thingamabob,
And dropped some coal onto the floor.
“You’re no longer on the nice list,
And this present soon you will miss.”
Not only had he crushed my dreams,
He ruined the whole rhyming scheme
And his cold, judgemental gleam
Did cause a rage never known before.
Time to even up the score.
“You will give what I asked for,
Every toy in the toy store
Or you will spend Christmas Eve
Bound and chained to my floor!”
Back toward the entrance turning,
All my soul within me burning
My adrenaline was churning
As I dead-bolted the door.
Sadly, it had come to this.
Obtaining my dad’s BB gun
In rampant anger, from the floor.

Getting gifts was such a chore.

"Empty the bag onto the floor."

"How dare you dare to threaten me,
For I am Santa Claus and you'll see
I can't be pressed to giving better gifts
Whenever you want more.
You little children need to learn,
That true respect is something earned.
The value of Christmas is the giving,
The spirit, the family and loving living!
Not all of this thoughtless lore!"

He was right, and as I saw
Society is forgetting the Christmas core
The spirit, the family and loving living.
A cup of kindness that we share with another,
A sweet reunion with a friend or a brother,
The giving of a gift to another
Tender caring that we share with a lover.
We need to think of what is shared
From the heart, love is prepared
It's not about profit or greed
It's for the spirit
And nothing more.

Merry Xmas! By Ethan Cooke age 11

The joy of Christmas by Amber Burton age 12, Rose Burton, age 12 Rebecca Mawbey age 11 & Megan Sargent age 11

My favourite time of year is here, full of laughter and great cheer.
I love the stockings on the wall, and all the sparkly baubles.
I hate the way the snow makes me shiver, but I love the warmth of the roast turkey dinner.
I love the Christmas tree big and bright, and white snowy houses glowing with light.
I hate the way the table is packed, but sure enough my presents are stacked.
My favourite time of year is here, full of laughter and great cheer.
I love the way the people sing, with huge crowds of people holding a grin.
I hate the way when the naughty elves come, they seem to think vandalising is a lot of fun.
I love the way the Christmas holidays are great, especially when we celebrate.
I hate that when my grandpa sits down, he starts to talk of his childhood town.
My favourite time of year is here, full of laughter and great cheer.
I love opening the calendar day after day, but then on the 26th it sadly gets put away.
I hate the way I'm the odd one out, not holding a present but a big brussel sprout.
I love the cheeky elf on the shelf, when I'm asleep he's his normal self.
I hate the fruity Christmas pud but I love the taste of the roast dinner spuds.
So come along to my sort of town, where the joy of Christmas is spread all around.

A Christmas Scene by Faye Jackson age 11

Merry Christmas Lulu by Kiera Wilton age 14

Christmas Eve 2072
It was Christmas Eve again, and as always Lulu was sat alone in the corner of the orphanage lounge. In her arms she held her old bear Mr Cuddles. She stared into his cold beady eyes and sighed.
"Please Santa. Give me a loving family."
Then she got and walked back to her dorm room slowly, knowing wishes were for 3 year olds.
Christmas Day 2072.
When Lulu woke up in the morning, she noticed Mr Cuddles was just…...gone.
"Maybe I left him downstairs or something"
So she got up, put on her Christmas dress, and started her search for him.
Kitchen. No one. Playground. No one. Dorm rooms. No one.
After spending about 7 minutes looking for him she sat on the sofa, tears falling down her face until……..
"SURPRISE LULU!!"
She jumped, but then turned around and saw the employees and two new adults holding her teddy Mr Cuddles.
"Welcome, my new daughter"
So wishes could come true.
Just one wish is all you need to help change the world.
If you wish for something, just wait and it will come true.

Christmas poem by Grace Day age 12

On Christmas Eve,
In bed we lay,
Waiting for the Christmas day,
When you start to see the light,
Get out of a bed without a fright,

Run into your parents room,
Dragging the stocking along with you,
When you've opened all your gifts,
Say thank you and make a wish,

When you run downstairs with glee,
Presents are all you see,
Parents tell you to wait there,
Too exited you just can't bear,

A Christmas lunch with broccoli,
Chicken, potatoes and green beans,
When all the foods been eaten up,
Take a drink from your cup

When the present exchanging is all done,
Play some games, have some fun,
Make a house of gingerbread,
Read a book you haven't read,

Eat some sweets after lunch,
Maybe a candy cane, munch, munch, munch
Light a candle on the fireplace,
Go outside and have a race,

Go sledge down a snowy hill,
Have a hot chocolate and chill,
Dunk a cookie in hot milk,

Wear a jumper made from silk,

When the day has come to an end,
You wish you could do it all again

Goodbye by Kimberley Bicknell age 16

Crystal's Christmas by Shannon Kingston age 11

Crystal lay shivering in the depths of the cavern in the Arctic cliffs. She was waiting impatiently for her Mother to come home after catching some food to eat. It felt like years had gone by before she heard the familiar footsteps prowl up to the entrance of the cave. Happily, she bounded forward to find out what was for dinner.

Instead of her kind mother, she saw a large figure dressed in red from head to toe. He had a long beard as white as snow and rosy cheeks which were almost as red as his clothes. On his shoulder was a humungous sack full of colourful shiny things. Crystal growled cautiously and bared her sharp teeth. The man looked at her with gentle eyes and said, in a lilting, jolly voice, "Don't worry little one. I mean no harm. Here, let's get you to a warmer place; you're freezing!" Then he bundled up the cub in a soft blanket and carried her onto his sleigh. "My name is Santa Claus," he said as he sprinkled some glittery powder on Crystal's head," What is yours?"

"I am Crystal." Suddenly a warm cosy feeling spread over her and she snuggled happily into his arms.

After a while, the snow and ice seemed to thaw, and they began to travel above grass. "Where are we?" asked a confused Crystal, "Are we lost?"

But Santa just smiled.

They flew over houses and chimneys until Santa said "We must stop here. I have something to show you."

Full of curiosity, the little polar bear glanced down at the roof below in wonder. What was Santa talking about? He leapt out of the sleigh with his sack full of colours and began to climb down the chimney. "What are you doing?" Crystal murmured with a puzzled expression. But Santa kept going. When they came to the bottom of the chimney, Crystal spotted a fir tree decorated with sparkling lights. Santa knelt down on the carpet and opened the giant sack. It was full of beautifully wrapped parcels. Without a sound, he lay them out under the tree and then shot back up the chimney followed by an extremely perplexed Crystal.

"What was all that about?"

Santa chuckled, "I was giving all the little boys and girls special presents for Christmas."

"Christmas? What is that?"

“It is when everyone gives presents and has a fun time with their family. On Christmas Eve, I give all the good children a special present as a reward for not being naughty.”

They carried on delivering presents all night until they arrived in a place called France. At first, they did the same as before: climb down the chute, lay out the presents and sprinkle a little festive magic. But things began to go wrong when they heard a noise from upstairs. Without a sound, they crept towards the hallway and spotted two young girls. The eldest had short brown hair and a white nightdress; the other had short gingery blond locks that fell just past her shoulders. The younger girl squealed in delight at the sight of Crystal then chattered loudly to her sister in a flurry of excited French. The brunette hushed her with a panicked look on her face; she didn’t want to wake her parents! The littlest child ran down the steps and scooped up the baby polar bear in her arms. Santa smiled as the girl spun round, her face full of pure joy. Carefully, she gave Crystal back to Santa and ran to her sister. Santa grabbed a fistful of magic and sprinkled it over the cub and the girl. The children sped up to bed without a second’s thought and then Crystal noticed a small parcel that she was sure was not there before. As she lifted the glittering lid, she noticed a beautiful snow globe with a miniature version of the two sisters and… herself. She knew the girls would treasure it forever.

After that, Crystal began to feel sleepy. She asked Santa if she could go home.
By the time they had reached the Arctic cliffs, Crystal had dropped off to sleep. She stirred awake and realised she was home. Inside the cave, she could hear her mother panicking and searching for her. Santa scooped up the cub and said “Goodbye Crystal. I will visit every year but first…”
Meanwhile, her mother was beside herself with worry after searching high and low. Out of the corner of her eye, she spotted a shimmery box with a purple ribbon on top. She untied the bow and outburst… Crystal! Crystal knocked over the box and ran to her mother. After a tearful reunion, Crystal explained what fun she had had that night and when at last she had finished her story, she went to sleep. Ever since, she has not forgotten Santa and she looks out at the night sky every Christmas Eve to see his sleigh flying through the air.
As for Santa, every Christmas Eve he visits Crystal and gives her special presents for being such a good cub all year.

A Secret Santa Cat by Rebecca Eastlake age 11

Our story starts on December 12th when Snowflake the cat was reading The Priory Times headlines. One of the headlines said…

Snowflake didn't hesitate to think. She had to save Christmas and create a freezing machine to get Santa back to the north pole. The problem was that the north pole was thousands of miles from where she was. The sea was freezing in December. She had to swim or take a different route.
Snowflake ran to Jones' Scrapyard and unearthed a solar panel that she remembered seeing once. She worked on it from about an hour and successfully converted into a freezing machine. She thought that test flights would cost her valuable time so she took off without any thoughts for her safety. Over the sea she saw whales, dolphins and more of nature's beauty. She spotted the ice floe that Santa's grotto was on. Snowflake did not want to be spotted so she hovered high in the sky and angled the solar panel at the sun.
The sunlight shone on to the solar panel and the machine began to do its work. Huge ice balls began to form in the sea filling the gap between Santa's ice floe and the icecap of the north pole.
Snowflake knew that he needed to finish his task before Christmas Eve so girls and boys could get their presents.
The machine took its time but Snowflake was determined to save Christmas

for everyone. The ice continued to form as the machine worked its magic. As clouds began to form blocking out the sunshine, snowflake realised that a blizzard was on its way. Snowflake flew higher but the clouds gathered faster and faster. Two hours later, just a tiny gap in the clouds was left. The freezing machine continued to freeze the ice as fast as it could. The dreaded thought of children crying on Christmas Day encouraged Snowflake to carry on. She fly higher and higher to gather the sunlight with just a little patch of water left to freeze.

The final piece of ice formed. Santa was saved but would never know that little Snowflake the cat had saved Christmas for everyone. Snowflake knew that she would keep the secret forever. Polar Bears became healthier as did all the other animals of the arctic. Santa was reunited with his home as Snowflake looked on feeling an enormous sense of relief.

Snowflake brought the machine back to England. She hid the machine in a safe place to help keep the secret that it was Snowflake the secret Santa cat that had saved Christmas.

A Christmas Story by Grace Durbin age 11

One cold night, a girl named Willow stepped outside one Christmas Eve morning. But this was not any morning, no because this is the day that one young Willow found Christmas…
Willow a brave young girl went outside in the snow and surprisingly whispered “Where am I? Mummy where are you?” to herself. She realised that she was lost.
Then out of nowhere a tall jolly man appeared behind her and whispered “come with me and I will help you”
Poor Willow was relieved to bump into this mysterious person. She knew in an instant that she was safe and followed him in his large house…
When she went inside, she saw nothing she never saw before. There was lollies, dollies and teddies too on that moment she realised
It was the one and only Santa Claus; a long white beard with a snowy look. Some dark blue eyes and a joy looking smile.
“Hi Willow” he said with a grin. “Now let’s get you home”.
Safely at home, Willow heard Santa say ”Ho Ho Ho merry Christmas everyone” before vanishing into the night.

Pie's Wish by Siyana Marinova aged 11 & Ellie Millard age 12

Once upon a time there lived Granny Christmas. She was Santa Claus' sister. Her job was to look after his reindeer until Christmas came and then he will take off to deliver presents to every child in the world. But, Granny Christmas had her own pet which was hers only. It was Pie a sheep. Granny Christmas decided on that name since Pie would always eat all the mince pies that would ever be laid on the table. Pie wasn't just an ordinary sheep though since whenever Granny Christmas took some wool from Pie it would re-grow back quickly when she ate magical polar grass.

It was getting near Christmas now. Santa's reindeer and Pie were inside the barn, talking about their Christmas wishes for this year.

"This year I want new reins because mine are getting old!" Said Comet excited to get glossy new reins with red glitter on them.

"I want some beautiful socks so that my hoofs are warm and cozy. "Said Dancer already imagining what colour the socks would be.

Pie looked joyfully at everyone, waiting for her turn to come to say her wish. No one knew about her wish because she didn't know who tell since it was really unusual for a sheep. Finally, Rudolph decided to ask Pie since she seemed kind of lonely.

"So Pie what's your Christmas wish for this year?"

"Well, my Christmas wish for this year is to become a reindeer! Just like you guys!"

Everyone became quiet. Then all the reindeer started laughing like never before including Rudolph who firstly showed sympathy to see what Pie's wish was.

"I'm sorry Pie but that's impossible!" shouted Blitzen at the top of everyone's laughter.

"Yeah even someone like Santa can't do this, that is too much." Cupid said trying to calm everyone down.

"Pie why are you wishing for this exactly?!" I mean wish for something useful like new colour wool or I don't know something cool you know?" asked Dasher.

"But this is cool for me!" demanded Pie to the others.

"Ok but just so you know that will never happen." said Donner.

"You will see anything can come true on Christmas!"

Pie lay down in her patch of hay and fell asleep, dreaming away.
Next day Pie woke up, remembering about her amazing dream of how she flew with the other reindeer and had giant greyish antlers which stood on her furry head. She felt positive today. It was Christmas day and Pie was waiting for Santa to come, she always loved those times.
Santa finally came, with his enormous white beard and his crimson jacket. He got all the reindeer out of the barn and put them on their reins. Then Santa spoke unexpectedly.
"Ah I almost forgot!" Santa exclaimed. "For a very special sheep!"
Pie looked over puzzled what Santa was talking about.
"It's you Pie! Now you can become a reindeer for 24 hours with all the extras. So make it the best you can, not everyone becomes a reindeer every day!"
Then Santa turned Pie into a majestic reindeer. Her top of the head to the neck fur was snow white and her bottom part of her back and legs was tinted light grey and large beige antlers which looked curled on her head.
"Hmm I wonder, do you want to come with us Pie?"
"What do you mean Santa?"
"I mean do you want to come and deliver presents with me this Christmas?"
Pie looked over at Granny Christmas. She didn't know what to do. She really wanted to go with Santa but she also felt guilty leaving Granny Christmas alone.
"Go Pie I won't mind I have work anyways so..."
“Thanks gran!” Pie (now the reindeer) ran over to Granny Christmas and nuzzled her head in her face.
"Now go, or you will be late!"
"Bye gran!"
Pie went to the front row and put her reins on. She was in the front row which meant loads of responsibility since the front row leads all the other reindeer. She took a deep breath and asked.
"Well how do you fly then?"
"Just jump and let your heart lead you." Replied Santa calmly.
Pie took a leap into the air and flew, away into the starry sky.

Pies Wish

Stuck inside by Libby Boneham age 11 & Erin Shepard age 11

Chapter 1. Flickering lights

The 23th December and two of my friends came over to my house for a sleepover. That night we decided to watch a Jolly Christmas film. To make us get more into the Christmas spirit of course. I sat down on my beanbag and all of a sudden, my beanbag popped and the beads went everywhere but I did not mind too much it looked like snow. Half an hour later, all the lights in the living room flickered and as soon as we knew it, we were in pitch black…I had the feeling that I was traveling in time or through space I couldn't really explain what it felt like unless you experienced it yourself.

Chapter 2. Unconscious

Slowly opening my eyes, I found myself laying on the freezing cold snow on my belly. I was freezing my friends and I were not dressed for this occasion. I looked around and saw Sophie and Emma looking down at me “yes! you are finally awake, but never mind that most importantly are you ok!” Emma worriedly said.
“yeah are you, Sophie replied, okay!”
I answered, “I think so my head hurts just a little bit, where are we?”
“I don’t know!” they both replied.

Chapter 3. The wonderland

Walking around we heard a gust of wind that came from nowhere and none of us knew what it was. Suddenly a snow storm began. We were doomed. No one had got out of a snow storm before. Soon after, I saw a red circle glowing brighter than ever. It came right up close to us and put us on their back and started to lift us off the floor. Gliding through the air, we were out in no time. I looked down and saw that it was a reindeer that had saved us. I saw that around its neck there was a name tag. I read the name tag on him and it said Rudolf. I was riding Rudolf!

Chapter 4. The board game

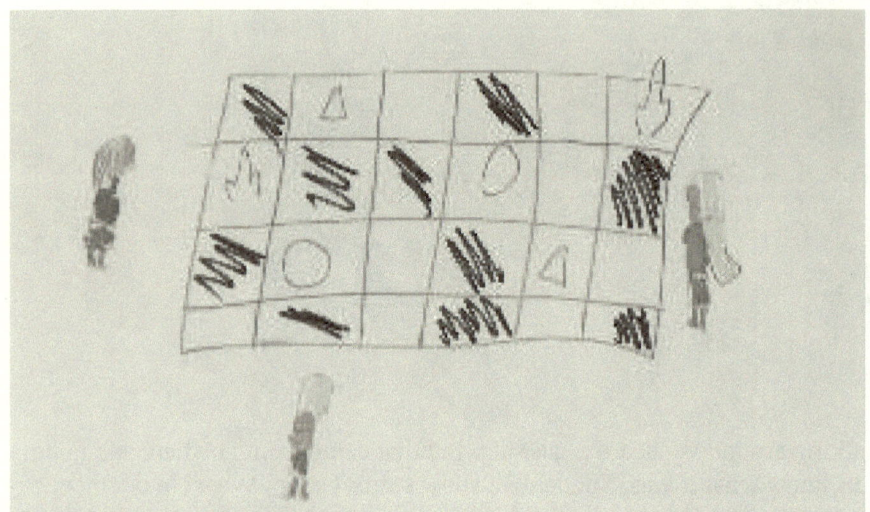

We asked the reindeer if they could take us to the exit and they did what we asked. A few minutes later, we landed I hopped off and found myself looking at a board game and a humongous door. The reindeer started to speak… "if you want to leave you have to play the board game to go through that door and you will go back home." We sat down on the cold snow and started to play the board game. We looked at the game, it looked like we had to save a polar bear from a floating iceberg. It looked like a team game, Sophie and I soon came up with a plan, using a boat and lots of rope. Emma had to lure the bear onto the boat with lots of sardines. Two hours later, we won the game and the huge gate opened and we walked into it.

Chapter 5. Back home

The same feeling started again when we were traveling through space and time, but when we got back this time, I was not on the floor which I was happy about. Everything was all back to normal as if we had never left. As soon as we got back to the living room, we sat down like nothing happened. We each gave each other a look of, did that really happen or was it a day dream?

Back in the moment by Alice Bird age 14

"You sit there dear and I'll get the turkey", were the last words I heard before the darkness swallowed me whole.

Darkness.

It squeezed my consciousness outwards between its thumbs. It crushed me, sending my emotions being rolled backwards and forwards until I was left lonely amongst nothing. Suddenly, reality hit me.

I was sat on an outside bench, in front of the shops waiting for my mum to come out with the turkey. She had somehow forgotten it. The past events of these last few months had sent my mother crazy making her forget about everything. But seriously, Christmas of all days really was the worst to forget a turkey!

I felt extremely disorientated, struggling to remember how I got here. It was as if I had been sucked into a vacuum and it had released me, letting me plummet down into a reality I somehow slotted into. My fingers and toes felt numb as I looked around my surroundings. I tried to stand up but my knees wouldn't let me as they buckled below me. Maybe it was the freezing cold getting to me.

It was an absolute surprise to me that a shop was open - today of all days. How can a shop be open on Christmas day? I will refuse to work, when I get older, on such a holy day and I would resign in a heartbeat if my boss said otherwise.

Although my family dynamics are incredibly messy – our church is the only place that brings us all together. We are a modest family with little opportunities and when we go to church, we all come together as one. My older sister, Nora, isn't a committed Christian, like my mother and I - but she really respects the power of community the church provides us with.

Ever since Dad passed away, the thought of going to church makes me feel happy. I feel like the chaos around us calms; I feel the spirit of my Dad is still with me and I feel like he had never gone.

I looked down at my lovely new watch. How can it take so long to buy a bit of turkey from a pretty much empty shop?

My watch looked perfect on my little wrist. It complimented my syrup-tanned wrist with its beautiful pastel violet colour. It has a little pineapple in the middle with its crisp green leaves pointing to the hours and minutes

around the clock's face. I really loved that watch, my sister Nora bought it for me. I appreciated it more coming from her because of the consideration she would've put into it picking it for me.
As I looked up from my watch my mother stood before me with a plate of turkey.
"Is that why you took so long?", I said with utter confusion, "You were waiting for the turkey to cook?"
"How else would the turkey cook? You knew I was cooking a turkey Mum"
I gawped at my mother with complete surprise. Did she just call me Mum?
"Well, would you like some turkey on your plate then Mum?"
She did it again!
"What are you talking about?"
I looked down at my feet and there laid a perfectly set table with glistening silver cutlery placed beside my plate.
My mother shook me gently.
"My are you in a daze? Please Mum, answer me", her voice was shaky and was picking up more alert.
I looked around and the familiar streets that surround me started to crumble away. Right before my eyes, nothing except a blur of smudged colours could be seen.
"What is going on?", I gasped.
My eyes rolled back and forth and back and forth…
The piercing sound, like an untuned instrument, echoed around my head.
Silence.
My last feelings were the numbness of doubt. The blackness was unpromising and I felt the deep loneliness rise inside of me. Time stood stationary like a dragged-out summer's afternoon.
I sat in front of a long table with a bunch of friendly faces all gawping at me with confusion and horror. There, at that table, sat my children and their partners. Next to them sat their children, my grandchildren, and food amongst the middle of the table which separated us all.
There was silence.
This time the silence was just an awkward, 'What shall we do now?' sort of silence.
"I'm back", I whispered through my thick embarrassment, "I'm sorry".
I had relapsed, again. It was the dementia, it had poisoned my memories and

reality, again. The best way to explain it is my memories become like a kaleidoscope. The familiar colours that surround you can be so easily manipulated into memories which really aren't there. As you travel through the twisting memories, further and further on, the less the shapes seem friendly, the more revealing dark truths lurk showing you what proper reality is.

But for now, I'm back. Back in the present – and the present makes me so much happier than in the past. I'm back in the moment. And I'm determined to enjoy this moment. Sat around a table with the people that mean the most to me. And it is Christmas time. Everyone is happy, there is plenty of noise – happy noise. A happy, noisy Christmas. Bliss.

Snowy Winter by Gemma Bicknell age 13

Little Robin red breast By Sky Galbraith age 11

Little robin red breast
Perched upon a tree
Feather soft like silk
Beak smooth and hard like rock
Snow sprinkling down upon its wings
Frost biting at its claws
but as soon as Winter comes to an end
Our little robin red breast
Sweet and small and quiet
Fly away our robin will
Singing all day through

Robin by Mia Lindsay age 12

A Christmas poem by Grace Durbin age 11

I woke up in the morning running down the stairs,
I look at the label but the present is the mares.
I open the window and it is snowing I say with glee,
Then I See a tricycle and guess what it is for me...
The story is changing and I will tell you why,
Coz I spot my nanny and she is holding ice cream pie.
“Mmm” she says “have you been good?”
“Of course I am!” looking like Robin Hood...
I open it up and I said “oh wow!”
“I will wear that sweater right nowwww…”
It was pink, purple, orange too,
Do you like these colours? well that is up to you...
Sorry but there is no time to rhyme
Peace out.

Christmas love by Grace Durbin age 11

Christmas is a day to share love,
Have a good time here and above.
Running in the snow with my friend,
It is a time I will remember up to the end.
Santa is here to bring some fun,
The Christmas people in the sun,
Merry Christmas everyone.
As I decorate the Christmas tree,
So that is what Christmas means to me.

It’s Santa! by Sophie Grace Robertson age 11

It was late on Christmas eve. All was dark. I was sleeping in my bed When I heard a thump. I woke up and shouted “SANTA SANTA!”. My mum came into my room and said in a tired tone “go to sleep or Santa won't give you your presents”. So I said “OK, I’ll go to sleep” and my mum went back to bed. But I couldn't get the thought of Santa out of my head. So when my mum and dad went back to sleep I snuck downstairs to the living room. To my surprise I saw a big fat figure wearing a red suit with a white beard and hair and black boots. IT WAS SANTA. I held my breath so I didn't scream with excitement but obviously Santa must of heard me because he turned around with a half-eaten cookie in his hand and put his index finger on his mouth and whispered “SSSSSShhhhhh”. Then he picked up a carrot from the plate of cookies and carrots. He gave me the carrot from his hand and said in a cheerful voice “go feed the reindeer”. I looked through the window and I saw many tall reindeer standing outside. so I threw the carrot outside and they ate it in seconds. I turned back to Santa and he said quietly “go back to sleep or you won’t get any presents, all you will get is a lump of coal in your stocking”. So I went to bed and slowly drifted off to sleep. I woke up on Christmas morning and there were presents everywhere. “Thank you Santa!” I said under my breath.

Christmas wish list by Grace Ford age 11

As the carols are sung,
And the church bells are rung,
There will be some who are alone,
They have no place to call home,
Just think about those who don't have as much as you,
Maybe donate a thing or two
and put some happiness into their Christmas,
Take a few minutes to think about them and their Christmas wish list...

Christmas Eve by Paige McCreadie age 12

Tweet, tweet, tweet
The robins sing as the glimmering snow shines and the moon beams at the merriest time of the year.
Christmas presents under the sparkling tree covered head to toe in glistening baubles.
As the clock strikes twelve the snow hits the window where the children inside are fast asleep dreaming of Old Saint Nick.

Christmas Magic by Lewis Clarke age 12

Cooper woke up one morning to a bright, sunny and glorious day. He leaped out of bed and sprinted down the stairs to a fresh new day. The excited boy opened the 20 on his advent calendar and made his breakfast. He sat and ate his breakfast when his doorbell rang and his mum opened it.

“Is this the home of Cooper?” an elf asked.

“Yes it is,” his mum answered.

“Ok, just to warn you, Cooper is on the bad list and he needs to try to get onto the good list by Christmas Day!” the elf replied.

“Oh ok, thanks,” she answered.

“Have a great day!” The elf said as he walked off. Cooper had heard everything:

“Mum,” Cooper said,” Do you know how I can get onto the good list?”

“Hmm, I’m not sure.” Maybe you could do some jobs around the house?” Cooper took that as a no and went to sister for answers.

“Bonnie, do you know how to get onto the good list?” Cooper said.

“No, go away,” his older sister answered. Cooper didn’t know what to do. He only had 5 days until Christmas and he was on the bad list! So he spent the next 3 day trying to figure out how to get onto the good list. His friends, teachers and neighbours were all asked if they knew how to get onto Santa’s good side. Even though Copper had asked loads of people, he still had no answers. He felt as if all hope was lost until he asked one of his neighbours the popular question.

“Ok, I’ll tell you” the old man with a red and black hat said, “ Grab an item from your Christmas tree and go straight north from here and eventually you’ll find a lovely little village. Santa will be in that village with his team of elves. Find an elf with a yellow feather in his hat, not a red one. Give him that item and say ‘I really care about Christmas’. Then he should tell Santa to put you on the good list.”

“Ok, thank you so much!” Cooper responded, already running back to his house. Back inside his house, Cooper picked a bauble from his Christmas Tree. This bauble had a picture of Santa on his sleigh over a village, with the stars shining in the background. So Cooper and his mum set out on their journey. The duo decided to ride their bikes there and bring some food along with them. As Cooper watched the snow falling onto the branches of trees, there were squirrels playing in the thick snow. The snow was coming down

as fast as steam coming out a train, the trees as high as the stars in the night sky. The open, frosted fields spread out far and wide. A farm could be spotted with the farmhouse having lights going from one corner to the other. Cows could be heard rummaging in their cow shed.
In the distance, a small village caught the corner of Cooper's eye. The garlands were hanging across the street and people were standing chatting, laughing and having a good time. A small cottage stood proud in the centre of the village. As they got closer, Cooper could see lots of elves hanging around the cottage with a que of people, waiting to go inside. There was an elf with a yellow feather in his hat standing at the end of the que.
"Mum, that's the elf!" Cooper exclaimed.
"Go and give him the bauble then," his Mum replied. Cooper walked cautiously up to the mysterious elf, hoping for the best.
Cooper tapped him on the shoulder and placed the bauble in his hand "I do care about Christmas."
"Alright, I'll have a chat with Santa about it," the elf responded.
"Thanks," Cooper said and strolled off back to his bike.
That very night, Christmas Eve night, Cooper heard his front door close. He saw a man with a red and black hat, the same as the old man's hat, walk off to his sleigh and ride off into the night.

The Joy of Christmas by Freya Grafton age 13

Its Christmas time
Hear the church bells chime
Does Santa think you've been naughty or nice
It's too late to ask his elf's for advice
The hanging of decorations and mistletoe
Leaving Santa a treat, Ho, Ho Ho
Go to sleep and no peeking
No listening for Santa's boots squeaking
The snow is falling on the ground
The magic of Christmas is all around
Time to celebrate the birth of our king
Giving presents tied with pretty string
Fun and laughter shared with loved ones
Just remember to thank those tons
Lights twinkle on the tree
How blessed at Christmas time are we?

The Christmas Robin by Mia Wickens age 11

"Finally time to get away from that freak." Said the bully looking in his direction. "Hey, Noah! Want to go to the park with me after school?" asked a voice behind him. Noah recognised his best friend, Lexi. "Sure, I haven't got anything else to do tonight," he replied. They both walked to the park with the cold autumn air travelling around them. While they were on the swings, Noah kept hearing noises from the big tree behind. He didn't want anything interrupting his occasional trip to the park so he decided to investigate. "Noah, what you up to back there?" shouted Lexi from the swings not looking up from her phone. "Hey! Get over here!" cried Noah, alarming Lexi and making her fall of the swing in the process. She scrambled to her feet and went to see what Noah was so worked up about. She saw an injured robin in the tree hollow. He scooped it up in his bruised hands and ran to his parents' house. "Wow. I never knew you could run that fast!" said Lexi not too far behind. "But where exactly are we going?" Noah was more focused on getting to the location but he managed to say a couple of words, "We are going to… my parents' house." The building slowly came into view over the horizon with the setting sun. Noah burst through the door and into the living room, where his parents spent most of their time. His parents looked at him with their eyes burning with anger. "Get that infected, wild animal out of here this instant!" shouted Noah's mother. Normally, he would be terrified of his parents and would follow their orders without thinking but he wanted to look strong to show Lexi that he wasn't scared. "No! I am not letting you control me this time!" his mother was furious. "Then get out!" Noah ran out of the living room and into the hallway. He lost his footing and cut his knee on the loose nail stuck on the creaky floorboards. With the robin still safely inside his hands, Noah looked up at his mother now carrying a tray above him. As soon as the tray was about to make contact, Lexi protected her best friend with her own body while risking her life at the same time. The object collided with her head instead of Noah. "Oh my goodness I'm so sorry Miss Crystal!" said Noah's mother. Lexi grabbed Noah's hand and rushed out of the front door into the cold air. "How are you alive?" asked Noah still in shock. "That must of been a hard hit!" Lexi carried on running but managed to say some language. "I swear on the Christmas gods that that robin is powerful. I can feel it and now I understand why your hands are bruised" Noah went silent and didn't realise they ran through another door possibly belonging to Mr and Mrs Crystal. "Mother, help!" cried Lexi from the grand hallway. Noah was shocked to see Taylor Crystal and Justin Crystal, the famous celebrities running to Lexi's entrance. "Oh my goodness let's get you two cleaned up then" said Lexi's father taking them to the kitchen but Noah didn't move. "It's okay, sweetheart. Don't be afraid" said Lexi's mother gently. Noah felt comforted and followed Lexi's father into the kitchen. "What's that in your hands?" asked Justin (Lexi's father). Noah slowly opened up his hands showing the injured robin still happily sat in his hands. Relief flowed through him as he realised that the robin was still alive after the disaster. After they got cleaned up ,Taylor (Lexi's mother) spoke, "Well, I think it's time you should be getting back sweetie." Lexi went to his rescue and replied "His parents are on holiday so he doesn't have anywhere to stay so can he stay here for a while?" Taylor gladly agreed and Lexi took Noah to his bedroom. They said their goodbyes and parted ways. As the clock struck twelve, Noah heard voices coming from the kitchen. He got out of his warm duvet and tiptoed to the source of the voice. "If I just get up here then I can escape…" said the voice as Noah got closer to the kitchen. Noah turned on the light to see the robin on the counter… "Oh goodness don't scare me like that! Anyways, hello my name is Robin your friendly Christmas spirit!" said the robin. Noah looked at Robin shocked. "So you’re a robin called Robin, you are apparently a Christmas spirit and you can talk?" "Well...yes what's so surprising about that?" Noah looked at him confused and replied, "Birds don't talk here and there are no Christmas spirits." "Look here bud…my name is Noah." "Fine then Noah, when you found me in that tree hollow, I was just fighting the evil souls that want to destroy Christmas. They are coming in a couple of minutes so I need to get out of here." Noah hesitated to respond but bravely said back, "Can I help?" Robin was glad, "Of course we need all the help we can get. Let's go save Christmas!" shouted Lexi listening into the conversation all this time. They all quietly went out the front door, illuminated by the stars in the midnight sky. Snow started to fall as the darkness gathered together. It became two shadows known as the Evil Souls. "So decided to bring some friends today, Robin. We both know you’re weaker this year." Robin held his ground against the larger shadow's insult. "We're not afraid of you!" shouted Robin proving that he was strong. "Let's see how good your friends are at defending you!" The snow started to fall faster and all they could see was snow. Noah desperately tried to look through the whistling white wall but there was no sight of Robin or Lexi. His ears started ringing then...crash. Darkness… Lexi opened her eyes to see the snow was gone. She hopped to her feet and to her surprise she was smaller than before. Lexi heard Noah's screech behind her. "Lexi, Robin, where are you?!" "Noah! Over here!" she shouted back. Lexi looked at the bird standing in front of her. "Who are you and what did you do to Noah?" cried Lexi. "What do you mean? I am Noah but look at yourself you look… different." She rushed over to the frozen puddle. A robin looked back at her. "What!? No, I look weird!" "Lexi I think you look great" Noah said to comfort her. "OK enough talking, more fighting!" said Robin not too far behind them. "First step is learning to fly. We need to fly high into the sky to gather magic and defeat the Evil Souls." Robin explained and in no time, the pair were experts at flying. The Evil Souls appeared again but the smaller shadow laughed at them "Pathetic little Christmas birds can't do anything!" They all flew into the sky like Robin instructed and snow started to fall around them. "I, Robin the Royal Christmas spirit, command you to leave immediately!"

The snow hit the two shadows and shortly after they were gone till next Christmas. "Thank you for helping me with the annual fight. I couldn't have done it without you both" Robin said thankfully but Lexi wasn't paying attention. "Hey what's that glowing orb over there because it's kind of getting larger?" Lexi said slightly worried. In a flash of light, they were all turned back into their human forms, including Robin. "Wow, Robin, I never knew you looked like that!" Robin looked embarrassed at Noah's compliment. "I give you this charm that will take you to the Christmas Land anytime and will make you a Christmas spirit allowing you to turn into a Christmas animal at any time."

For proof, Robin turned into a snowy fox and Lexi and Noah looked surprised. "Give it a go. All you have to do is imagine an animal and it'll work" Noah turned into a wolf and Lexi turned into a white cat. They looked at Robin with wide eyes saying "Thank you!" "Well I think it's time we part ways don't you think." Robin said shaking the snow of his fur. "Noah, I thought you disappeared!" cried a voice behind Noah. He turned around to see his parents running towards him. His mother gave him a big hug. "I am so sorry, darling. Those mean shadows brainwashed us."

"Bye Noah!" Shouted Lexi walking away. "See you at school tomorrow!"

Years later, Robin, Lexi, and Noah are still fighting the Evil Souls every Christmas. "So that's our story isn't it Noah?" said Lexi to her two children Nixon and Lux. Lux looked at her mother with wide eyes. "So maybe we can hold the power you and Father has?" she said. "Well mine is going to be better!" said Nixon giving his little sister a gentle push. Noah chuckled, "Maybe you already have that power" he said. A few seconds later, Robin bursts through the door shouting, "Merry Christmas!"
To this very day, the same power is still out there. Someone just needs to believe...

Crystal and the Four Seasons by Katie Campbell age 11

It was a cold winters' day and Crystal, a young,11-year-old girl from England, was fighting with her siblings over who got to eat the last waffle for breakfast, as usual.
"I should have it because I'm the only one who does their chores!" Crystal shouted, pushing her shoulder-length, honey-blonde hair out of her bright, emerald-green eyes.
"As if! You haven't helped clean our room in days! And anyway, I am the smartest, so nobody can argue with me!" Crystal's sister, Ruby, exclaimed.
"You? The smartest? As if! I'm the oldest so I should get it!" Jacob – Crystal's older brother – bellowed, as he stormed to the cupboard and grabbed the single waffle. He was approaching the toaster when, out of nowhere, a tiny girl sprinted into the kitchen, wailing like a banshee, followed by a much calmer mother.
"What is all this screaming for? I said last night that Poppy was getting the last waffle and you three are getting toast! Now I would behave myself if I were you, or you might be grounded!" the mother sternly told the siblings, before taking the waffle and putting it in the toaster. Jacob stomped upstairs with an excellent impersonation of an elephant. He was followed by Ruby, who retired to the bathroom, and finally Crystal, who decided to opened her advent calendar.

As it was the first of December, Crystal was yet to open her advent calendar, and was excited to see what it was like, as every calendar was different. As she retreated to the room she shared with Ruby, she crept towards her bed, and retrieved the advent calendar from underneath it. Looking at it, she noticed a strange picture on the front, as it seemed to show all the seasons rather than just winter, as most advent calendars do. She scanned the calendar again and located the first door. As she lifted her hand to open it, she felt a strange sensation, like something not quite of this world. She prised the door open and instead of finding a chocolate inside, there was just a small picture of a snowflake. Suddenly, she felt as if she had been lifted off her feet and, dropping the calendar, felt as though she was being sucked into it.

Crystal opened her eyes to a small village full of bustling people. She rose to her feet and tried to ask them for help. Nobody seemed to take notice of her,

and she was knocked down again by the crowd, until a boy helped her back onto her feet. Crystal looked up at the mysterious boy with curiosity, and spoke quietly:
"Thank you. And, who are you exactly?"
The stranger spoke. "Jack. My name is Jack. What is yours?"
"Crystal." Crystal answered, taking in Jack's features: broad shoulders, a tall build, paper-white skin, frosty white hair and piercing, icy-blue eyes.
"What are you doing here?" Jack asked, looking startled. "I've never seen you here before."
"Well this is the problem. I have no idea where I am, and need some help getting home." Crystal explained.
Jack looked confused. "But you're supposed to be here! We need you!"
Now Crystal was also confused. "What do you need me for?"
Jack sighed. "A few thousand years ago, there was a diamond that controlled the climate and environment. A jealous queen shattered the gem, hoping to seize control over the world. Instead the gem broke into four parts that each controlled the four seasons. Each part has a guardian that is supposed to keep peace, but spring, summer and autumn are growing weaker and losing to winter. According to the story, the saviour of the seasons is named Crystal. If you don't do something, the world will be lost in eternal winter!"
With that, Crystal's world started spinning, and the next thing she knew, she was back home.

Crystal had returned to her home, exactly where she had been before, hand hovering over the first door in the advent calendar. It seemed as if no time had passed, and nobody had noticed her disappearance. She decided to go about her day as usual, all the while pondering what would happen tomorrow.

The next day, Ruby had already gone to school when Crystal awoke. Once she came to her senses, she leapt out of bed and sprang to her calendar with the force of a firework. Crystal prised open the second door and felt the strange flying sensation again. She landed in the same place, keeping her eyes open for Jack, when a voice behind her made her jump. "Here you are! I've been searching for you for hours!" Jack cried, relieved. "Where did you go?"
"I went home" Crystal replied. "Anyway, we need to do something about winter! We need to save the seasons!"

“Well then, we need to discuss our plan of action. Once we have prepared, we should be sent to the next world.” Jack stated, before he and Crystal began to plan out their journey. By the time Crystal had to go home, the two had already planned what to do for the next few days and Crystal was excited to put the plan into action. Or so she thought.

The third day of December, Crystal was sent to a new world she hadn't seen before. It was full of vibrant colours and sweet smells, warm sun and the sound of animals in the surrounding trees. A few metres away, in a small cyclone of snowflakes, Jack appeared over a small patch of dead grass and frost. Once he landed, he opened his eyes and took in his surroundings, before his eyes landed on her.
“You're here! Already? How?” he questioned, looking puzzled.
“I don't know. Do you have any idea where we are?” she replied.
Jack answered, “We are in the land of spring. We need to locate the crystal and retrieve it before you get sent somewhere else. Now, how do we find the crystal?”
As if on cue, the tree in front of the two began to glow. Crystal, looking surprised, alerted Jack.
“It's glowing! The tree is glowing!” she exclaimed, looking terrified.
Jack turned to the tree, as the trunk began to split in two. Out of the light, a small figure appeared, no taller than Crystal. It stepped out of the trunk and the tree healed up instantly. The figure solidified, taking on a human appearance. It had olive-coloured skin, blonde hair, and eyes that shifted between every shade of green. It looked decidedly female. She also had pointed ears, like an elf, with leaves and flowers woven into her hair. She looked up and spoke in a sweet, sing-song voice:
”Hello, saviours of our world. I am so glad you have come to our aid at this time of peril. My name is Flora, messenger of the seasons, guardian of the plants. I have been sent to lead you back to the Guardian of Spring, so she can tell you about the location of the gem of spring. Now, follow me.”
She turned, and walked back into the tree trunk. Before she disappeared into the light, she looked back. “Are you coming?” Crystal looked at Jack, bewildered, before he gestured to Flora, and Crystal stepped into the light.

She felt the floating sensation again, and, with Jack by her side and Flora leading the way, they materialised in a grand hall. It had to be as wide as a football pitch back home, she thought, and twice as long. The hall was full of green plants, small animals, and flowers every colour of the rainbow. At the other end, on an immense throne, surrounded by hundreds of animals, was a youthful-looking girl that Crystal assumed must be the Queen of Spring. As the trio approached the crowd, Crystal saw the Queen's fair skin, white hair, leaf-green eyes and happy expression. They had almost reached the throne, when Flora spoke.

"My Queen, I have brought the saviours as you requested. They wish to know where to find your crystal."

"Thank you Flora. Your work is much appreciated." the Queen told Flora. Then she turned to Crystal and Jack and, in a much less regal tone, explained: "I've been so worried. Flora said that you had arrived in the other world two days ago and I've been waiting to see you. You have four more days until you are sent to the next world. In order to ensure success, you must..."

But Crystal couldn't hear the rest of what the queen was saying, as she was being sent back home.

She could barely wait until the next morning, but feared she would destroy the magic if she opened a door too early. So each day, when Crystal woke up, she sprang out of bed to help Jack in saving the seasons and stopping the one responsible for all of the corruption of power and for unbalancing the laws of nature. Whoever that was.

The next two days in the advent calendar were spent planning what to do, which left two days to travel to the Mountain of Thorns (which was where the gem was being held). Everything was going well, until Crystal, Jack and Flora-who had been sent to ensure the safety of the two younger ones-were held up by a terrifying warrior. It was unbelievably tall, with a stocky build and sky-blue eyes, only visible through slits in the jet-black helmet it was wearing to go with the rest of the jet-black armour it was wearing. Crystal couldn't tell if it was a boy or a girl, until it spoke.

"I have been sent to take you to the castle," he said, "There my master will help you find the season crystals". Crystal was about to follow the man, until Jack leant closer to Flora and whisper something in her ear. Flora's face lit up with realisation, and she nodded to Jack. Suddenly, Jack grabbed Crystal's arm and shot to the side, as the warrior lunged forward and tried to grab her; instead he just grabbed air. The three weaved through bushes of thorns and boulders, followed by the hunter, until, finally, they were at the summit of the mountain. Before them stood an ancient temple, with a pedestal in the centre. On the pedestal, glowing green with an eerie light, there was-

“The crystal” Flora breathed, stepping closer. She edged closer to the crystal, hand outstretched, as the hunter barrelled through a bush behind them. As he took in the scene before him, his eyes glowed with fury: he hurtled forwards, about to crash into Crystal, when flora took the Spring crystal and the three dissolved into light. Crystal opened her eyes, and was hone, heart racing and full of adrenaline.

When crystal made her way into the calendar the next day, she was greeted with a blast of hot air and sunshine. She opened her eyes to endless fields of grass and sunflowers. Nearby, Jack materialised out of light, and Flora appeared a few metres away with a stranger beside her. The newcomer had much darker skin than Flora, with dark, earthy brown hair, and chocolatey brown eyes. Peeking out from her hair were two deer ears and a pair of small antlers. Flora approached Jack and Crystal and introduced the newcomer.

“This is Fauna. She is here to help and we usually work together.” Flora explained, looking excited to work with Fauna. “Our next task is to get you to the Palace of Summer. It is just over the hill.”

After the four made it to the Palace, Crystal stopped to admire the four towering spires, decorated in plants and flowers, and hundreds of intricate carvings and decorations. She snapped herself back to reality and stepped inside.

The throne room of this palace was very different to the previous one. Instead of being full of animals it was almost empty, with only two thrones and a table. In the largest throne sat who Crystal thought must be the Guardian of Summer. She was tall and striking, with velvety dark skin and hair. Almost as soon as the door behind them closed, the Queen leapt from her throne and strode across the room, looking thrilled to see them, and began to speak with a regal, commanding voice: “I'm glad you are here on time. It will take you days to reach the Summer crystal, so the sooner you leave the better. You must travel through the sunflower fields, until you reach the Valley of the Sun, then you should see the Temple where the crystal is. Nobody has been able to open the temple in the last dimension apart from you, so we need you to complete this mission. Now go!”

After three days of travelling, Crystal, Jack, Flora and Fauna arrived at the temple, but it was being guarded by the hunter Crystal encountered in the world of Spring, except this time he had olive green eyes. He looked up. His eyes widened at what he saw, and he charged. The four travellers dived out of the way, as the hunter flew past them like an enraged bull. Jack stood up and ran for the temple, with the hunter close behind. He grabbed the crystal just as the hunter was about to seize him, and he disappeared in a shower of bright light, before the others disappeared too.

The next world Crystal entered was very different to the other two. She was surrounded by leaves in a hundred different shades, from red to yellow, and orange to brown. She could hear the sound of animals rustling about in the mountain of leaves, and there was an overpowering smell of earth in the air. This time, the first person Crystal saw was not Jack, but the hunter, this time with brown eyes instead of blue or green. Crystal started to wonder why the eye colour changed for each world, but pushed the thought aside. She tried to stay quiet to avoid the hunter noticing her, as she was on her own. After a few minutes the hunter left, and Crystal saw Jack, Flora and Fauna come out from hiding behind the trees. They quickly discussed a plan, before Flora led the way to the Queen of Autumn. Instead of a palace, they found this queen in a forest glade, discussing something with a deer. When the queen noticed the four visitors she gestured for them to sit down, before dismissing the deer. She was sat cross-legged on the carpet of leaves, with her black, shoulder-length, tightly curled hair framing her tanned skin and earthy brown eyes. When she spoke, her voice was soft and melodic. “Thank you, for bringing them here.” She nodded to Flora and Fauna. “Now, this journey will be the most difficult so far, so listen closely.” After the queen finished, she quickly sent the four on their way. It took the rest of the day to finish the first part of the journey, and another four days to reach the temple, but they did so without much trouble, despite crossing paths with the hunter several times. Eventually, Crystal made it home with ease.

It was the twentieth of December, and the first day Crystal would spend in the land of Winter. When she arrived in winter, Jack, Flora and Fauna were already waiting for her. Without any explanation, the others turned and started walking away. Crystal tried to ask what was going on.

“Hey guys! What-”
“Be quiet” Jack whispered. ”They will hear you!”
“Who?” Crystal asked in a whisper.
“Everyone. The hunters, the Queen, the warriors. Everyone here is against us!” Flora replied.
“We know where to go, we just need to get there. And that's the hard part.” Fauna explained.
“Why? Where is the crystal?” Crystal asked.
“Well,, we don't know exactly.” Flora added.
“But where is it?” Crystal pressed.
“In the Castle of Winter.” Jack replied.
The rest of the journey was spent in silence.

Once the four reached the palace, they heard three low voices behind them.
“What did the queen tell us to do when we captured the 'saviours'?” The highest voice spoke.
“I don't know. Something about taking them and their companions to the palace.” replied the second voice. ”She did say she wanted them alive. And don't let the boy get away.”
“Stop yapping and get them!” The third, and lowest, voice ordered. Crystal turned, and saw three hunters; one with blue eyes, one with green eyes and the largest one had brown eyes. Now Crystal understood why the hunter had three different eye colours. They were three different people. She saw the leader lunge towards her and everything went black.

When Crystal opened her eyes again, she was in a grand throne room, with arches and statues made entirely of ice. In an intricately decorated throne sat the Queen of Winter. She seemed tall, and had jet-black hair that contrasted with her paper-white skin. Her icy blue eyes seemed to cut straight through you. Perched on her head was a delicate crown of ice, and in her hand she held a staff with what looked like a crystal of ice at the top. Crystal turned to look at the others and check that they were okay. Flora and Fauna were standing by the throne. Crystal guessed this was because they served *all* the seasons. Jack was beside Crystal and was looking at the Queen with a stare of pure hatred. The Queen spoke in a cold tone. “So, You have come to restore balance to the world of the seasons. Unfortunately, you will fail in your mission, so you should just stop trying to evade us.”

“Fat chance.” Jack growled.

Jack thrust out his hand and launched a horde of ice spikes at the Queen, before she retaliated with an army of snowballs. Jack yelled out to Flora and Fauna.
“Watch out! The hunters are going for you!” he cried, as he launched another wave of spikes at the Queen. Crystal turned, as Flora made a wall of plants to block the hunters from getting them. Crystal looked back to Jack, fighting the Queen, and then to the Queen, shooting attack after attack out of her staff. Crystal looked closer at the staff. The handle of ice... the carving on the staff... the ice crystal at the top... Crystal looked closer at the crystal. Was it made out of ice? Something in Crystal's memory tugged at her. Something Jack had said on the way to the castle. Something about the location of the Crystal of Winter... Crystal snapped back to reality. Of course! The Crystal of Winter was the crystal at the top of the staff! With the queen distracted, Crystal raced past Jack and began to pull the staff away from the Queen. She looked outraged, and tried to pull it back.
“What are you doing!” she screeched. “This is mine!”
“No it is not!” Crystal exclaimed defiantly and, with one final pull, she dislodged the crystal from the staff. Both people shot backwards, Crystal into Jack and the Queen into the wall.

Crystal felt her feet being lifted off of the ground and the air rushed around her, as the three other Seasons Guardians appeared: Spring, looking excited, Summer, looking relieved and Autumn, looking proud. Each held up their own crystal, and all four floated up, fused together and shrank into a necklace that fastened itself around Crystal's neck. As she landed, Summer spoke;
“You are now the peace keeper for the Seasons. The necklace allows you to travel to any of the Season dimensions, as well as any of the middle worlds, such as your home world.” Behind Crystal, the Queen of Winter stirred. Jack walked over to her. “You are banished from this world and any other Season world.” he commanded. Crystal turned to Summer again.
“Is Jack allowed to do that?” She questioned.
Summer replied, “Well, as he is the rightful King of Winter, I think Jack Frost is allowed to do that.”
Crystal stared at Jack in disbelief. “What?!”
Jack smiled. “What next?”

Crystal laughed. “Let's start by fixing the damage the old queen did.” Crystal, Jack, Spring, Summer, Autumn, Flora and Fauna spent the rest of the day discussing their plan of action.

The next month was spent fixing the damage and introducing everyone to the new King of Winter and Seasons Keeper. After this, Crystal would visit the others once a month, and she looked forward to it every time. She was ready to do anything to keep the seasons in balance, and was waiting for the next adventure to begin, the question was, what would the next adventure be?

www.ingramcontent.com/pod-product-compliance
Lightning Source LLC
LaVergne TN
LVHW040925150826
845672LV00007B/2199

* 9 7 9 8 7 5 5 0 8 2 9 5 2 *